Ma

by Murray Ogilvie

Lang**Syne**
PUBLISHING
WRITING *to* REMEMBER

Lang**Syne**

PUBLISHING

WRITING *to* REMEMBER

Vineyard Business Centre,
Pathhead, Midlothian EH37 5XP
Tel: 01875 321 203 Fax: 01875 321 233
E-mail: info@lang-syne.co.uk
www.langsyneshop.co.uk

Design by Dorothy Meikle
Printed by Montgomery Litho, Glasgow
© Lang Syne Publishers Ltd 2011

All rights reserved. No part of this publication may be reproduced, stored or introduced into a retrieval system, or transmitted in any form or by any means (electronic, mechanical, photocopying, recording or otherwise) without the prior written permission of Lang Syne Publishers Ltd.

ISBN 978-1-85217-291-6

MacCallum

ASSOCIATED NAMES INCLUDE:
Allum
Callam
Callum
Challum
Macallum
MacCalim
MacCallome
MacCalme
MacCaluim
MacCalume
MacColem
MacColum
MacCollom
MacCollum
MacCullom
MacCullum

MacCallum

MOTTO:
In ardua tendit
(He has attempted difficult things).

CREST:
A Tower.

TERRITORY:
Argyll.

Chapter one:

The origins of the clan system

by Rennie McOwan

The original Scottish clans of the Highlands and the great families of the Lowlands and Borders were gatherings of families, relatives, allies and neighbours for mutual protection against rivals or invaders.

Scotland experienced invasion from the Vikings, the Romans and English armies from the south. The Norman invasion of what is now England also had an influence on land-holding in Scotland. Some of these invaders stayed on and in time became 'Scottish'.

The word clan derives from the Gaelic language term 'clann', meaning children, and it was first used many centuries ago as communities were formed around tribal lands in glens and mountain fastnesses.

The format of clans changed over the centuries, but at its best the chief and his family held the land on behalf of all, like trustees, and the ordinary clansmen and women believed they had a blood relationship with the founder of their clan.

There were two way duties and obligations. An inadequate chief could be deposed and replaced by someone of greater ability.

Clan people had an immense pride in race. Their relationship with the chief was like adult children to a father and they had a real dignity.

The concept of clanship is very old and a more feudal notion of authority gradually crept in.

Pictland, for instance, was divided into seven principalities ruled by feudal leaders who were the strongest and most charismatic leaders of their particular groups.

By the sixth century the 'British' kingdoms of Strathclyde, Lothian and Celtic Dalriada (Argyll) had emerged and Scotland, as one nation, began to take shape in the time of King Kenneth MacAlpin.

Some chiefs claimed descent from

ancient kings which may not have been accurate in every case.

By the twelfth and thirteenth centuries the clans and families were more strongly brought under the central control of Scottish monarchs.

Lands were awarded and administered more and more under royal favour, yet the power of the area clan chiefs was still very great.

The long wars to ensure Scotland's independence against the expansionist ideas of English monarchs extended the influence of some clans and reduced the lands of others.

Those who supported Scotland's greatest king, Robert the Bruce, were awarded the territories of the families who had opposed his claim to the Scottish throne.

In the Scottish Borders country – the notorious Debatable Lands – the great families built up a ferocious reputation for providing warlike men accustomed to raiding into England and occasionally fighting one another.

Chiefs had the power to dispense justice

and to confiscate lands and clan warfare produced a society where martial virtues – courage, hardiness, tenacity – were greatly admired.

Gradually the relationship between the clans and the Crown became strained as Scottish monarchs became more orientated to life in the Lowlands and, on occasion, towards England.

The Highland clans spoke a different language, Gaelic, whereas the language of Lowland Scotland and the court was Scots and in more modern times, English.

Highlanders dressed differently, had different customs, and their wild mountain land sometimes seemed almost foreign to people living in the Lowlands.

It must be emphasised that Gaelic culture was very rich and story-telling, poetry, piping, the clarsach (harp) and other music all flourished and were greatly respected.

Highland culture was different from other parts of Scotland but it was not inferior or less sophisticated.

Central Government, whether in London

"The spirit of the clan means much to thousands of people"

or Edinburgh, sometimes saw the Gaelic clans as a challenge to their authority and some sent expeditions into the Highlands and west to crush the power of the Lords of the Isles.

Nevertheless, when the eighteenth century Jacobite Risings came along the cause of the Stuarts was mainly supported by Highland clans.

The word Jacobite comes from the Latin for James - Jacobus. The Jacobites wanted to restore the exiled Stuarts to the throne of Britain.

The monarchies of Scotland and England became one in 1603 when King James VI of Scotland (1st of England) gained the English throne after Queen Elizabeth died.

The Union of Parliaments of Scotland and England, the Treaty of Union, took place in 1707.

Some Highland clans, of course, and Lowland families opposed the Jacobites and supported the incoming Hanoverians.

After the Jacobite cause finally went down at Culloden in 1746 a kind of ethnic cleansing took place. The power of the chiefs was curtailed. Tartan and the pipes were banned in law.

Many emigrated, some because they wanted to, some because they were evicted by force. In addition, many Highlanders left for the cities of the south to seek work.

Many of the clan lands became home to sheep and deer shooting estates.

But the warlike traditions of the clans and the great Lowland and Border families lived on, with their descendants fighting bravely for freedom in two world wars.

Remember the men from whence you came, says the Gaelic proverb, and to that could be added the role of many heroic women.

The spirit of the clan, of having roots, whether Highland or Lowland, means much to thousands of people.

12 — *The origins of the clan system*

Clan warfare produced a society where courage and tenacity were greatly admired

Chapter two:

Saintly origins

The origin of the name MacCallum can be traced all the way back to the arrival in Scotland of St Columba from Ireland.

Columba was a pupil at a monastic school at Clonard Abbey, which is found in modern County Meath. Twelve students who studied there became known as the Twelve Apostles of Ireland. Columba was one of these. He became a monk and was ordained as a priest. Around the year 560, he was involved in a dispute over a manuscript. This disagreement led to the Battle of Cúl Dreimhne in 561, during which many men were killed. A synod of clerics and scholars threatened to excommunicate him for these deaths, but he was allowed to go into exile instead. Columba suggested that he would work as a missionary in Scotland to help convert as many people as had been killed in the battle. He settled in Iona and is regarded as the man who brought Christianity to

Scotland. The Gaelic versions of MacCallum are Mac Chalium or Maol Chalium. They are translated as devotee or son of Columba. There is no evidence to suggest a blood relationship so it is generally accepted that the original MacCallum was a close follower of St Columba.

Chapter three:

Curse on the clan

Nearly 900 years after the time of St Columba would pass before an official record of the MacCallums would exist.

They had been living peacefully in a part of Argyll known as the Lorne. The clan seat was in Colgin, a few miles outside Oban. Descendants of these MacCallums were involved in a legendary incident which could have been considered comical, had it not resulted in a large number of needless deaths. In the fourteenth century, according to the story, the Laird of Colgin has 12 sons. One day a woman of the MacDougall clan who lived locally placed a curse on his family. The boys began to die and eventually only three were left. Their father, desperate to save his surviving sons, decided to send them away from home. He saddled up three horses and placed a bag with food and possessions on each. The three boys were given a horse each and told to leave and make their future wherever the bag fell off the horse.

One bag fell off on MacCallum's land so the first boy stayed at home. The second boy ended up in Glenetive, northeast of Oban while the third headed south and settled in Kilmartin, which is between Oban and Lochgilphead. The boys married and had families. Their families multiplied and through time became quite sizeable.

One day a group of 30 Glenetive MacCallum men decided to visit their cousins in Kilmartin. Coincidentally, the Kilmartin branch decided to visit their cousins on the same day and 30 of them set off. The two groups, who were not acquainted with each other, met at a narrow Highland pass and neither would move aside to allow the other to go through.

Before long tempers flared and a full scale pitched battle erupted. Only two men survived, one from each side. Exhausted by the conflict they agreed to sit down and have a rest from fighting. During the course of the conversation it emerged they were related. From that moment on the MacCallums became known as "The descendents of the 60 fools".

There is another version of this legend for which, historically, there is a degree of proof. This time, so the story goes, the Chief of the MacCallums had 12 sons, one of whom was wanted by the wife of a nearby laird. The chief refused to entertain her and in response she cast an evil spell on them. One by one they began to die until only three boys were left. The father, fearing for their safety, ordered each to fill two saddlebags with possessions and supplies. He then bound together heather to make ropes and tied the saddlebags onto three horses. His sons were sent on their way and told to keep riding south until the ropes tore and the saddlebags slipped. The first son's bags fell off at Kilmartin near Lochgilphead. He settled there and to this day there are McCallum families in this area. The present clan Chief lives at Duntrune Castle near Kilmartin at the edge of a rocky promontory on the shore. The second son ended up at the village of Clachan, in Kintyre, about ten miles south of Tarbert, Loch Fyne. His descendants settled in the area and still live there. The third brother continued down Kintyre. As he passed Campbeltown, he saw the sea coming into view and began wondering if he was destined to end up in the water! But 100 yards from the beach his rope finally snapped and he started his new life at Southend. The McCallum family are well known in the area. They include Ronald McCallum who was the personal piper to the Duke of Argyll and a number of highly-skilled and highly-thought-of tradesmen.

Chapter four:

Rebellion and retribution

Despite the proliferation of MacCallums in these three areas, it is the early part of the fifteenth century before official records make mention of them. By then the area was under the control of the mighty Clan Campbell and the MacCallums fell under their protection. In 1414 Sir Duncan Campbell of Lochow granted land in Craignish and on the banks of Loch Avich to Reginald MacCallum of Corbarron, who also took on the honour of Hereditary Constable of Castle Craignish on the western shore of Loch Craignish west of Kilmartin and the nearby Castle Lochaffy.

In 1510, Maol Caluim had a grant of the lands of Poltalloch, across Loch Craignish from the lands of Craignish Castle. He was succeeded by his son Archibald and by 1562 Donald, son of Archibald, was in possession of Poltalloch.

At that time there were several spellings

of the name. These included McAlchallum, McOlchallum and McAlchallam. The prefix "Al" is Gaelic for "son of" and until 1685 the clan members were happy to use it. But tumultuous events that year would bring about a change of name, the first of two such alterations to affect the MacCallums.

In the late seventeenth century Britain was split by religious rivalry. At the heart of it was the ruling House of Stuart. The MacCallums became caught up in two costly rebellions connected to the Stuarts.

In April, 1685 King Charles II was succeeded by his Roman Catholic brother, James II of England and VII of Scotland. Charles, a Protestant, had no legitimate heirs.

Many in the country were against a Catholic king. There was a great deal of support for Charles's first-born son, James Scott, a Protestant. He was the product of a liaison between Charles and Lucy Walter and although he was the king's favourite child he would not make him his heir. Scott was born in Holland. In

1663, at the age of 14, he arrived in England and was given the titles Duke of Monmouth, Earl of Doncaster and Baron Scott of Tynedale. He then married Anne Scott, the wealthy fourth Countess of Buccleuch. The couple became the first Duke and Duchess of Buccleuch. There had been rumours that Charles had married Monmouth's mother, Lucy Walter, but there was no evidence and Charles always swore he only had one wife, Catherine of Braganza.

Soon after becoming king, James faced a joint rebellion in Scotland led by Archibald Campbell, the Earl of Argyll, and in England led by the Duke of Monmouth. The rebels met in the Netherlands, where they planned their campaigns, and set sail from there.

Argyll landed at Campbelltown on May 20 and spent some days raising a small army of supporters, mainly from his own clan and those, like the MacCallums, who were loyal to it.

His plan of attack was to march south towards Glasgow and the lowlands where he could find a sizeable Presbyterian support. But forces in their thousands loyal to King James were chasing him from all sides. By mid-June at Kilpatrick on the banks of the River Clyde his band of men, numbering no more than 500, finally gave up and began dispersing in an attempt to save their own skins.

Argyll was captured on or just after June 18 and taken to Edinburgh where he was executed 12 days later. There was terrible retribution against the Campbells and their followers. Most lost their lands and possessions. Many were tortured and executed. A small number were sent to the West Indies as indentured slaves. It is at this point and to avoid those punishments that the MacCallums dropped the Gaelic spelling of their name.

South of the Border the rebellion by the Duke of Monmouth suffered an equally ignominious fate. He was captured and executed while his followers were subjected to a retribution so savage, it led to a national outcry — even among those who were loyal to the king.

The next time the MacCallums were

caught up in a rebellion, they sided against the rebel force of which they had previously been a part.

King James was deposed three years after the Duke of Argyll was executed. The religious split within the country refused to die down after the rebellions were crushed. If anything they intensified. Matters came to a head in 1688, when James fathered a son, James Francis Edward. Until then, the throne would have passed to his daughter, Mary, a Protestant. Threatened by a Catholic dynasty, several influential Protestants decided to take action. Their plan was to depose James and replace him with his daughter Mary and her husband, William Henry of Orange — both Protestants. William, who was also Mary's first cousin and, therefore, James's nephew, was the leading light of the Protestant cause against Catholicism in Europe. In November 1688 William set sail from his home in the Netherlands and invaded England. James, despite numerical superiority did not attack the invaders. This show of cowardice eventually led to a bloodless coup. James was allowed to escape to France and

William and Mary became joint rulers. They passed laws which ensured that the British monarchy would be forever Protestant.

There were still many Catholics in the country, particularly in the north of Scotland. And there were many, on both sides of the religious divide, who wanted the Stuarts back on the throne. They continued to foment rebellion and in 1715 they got one. James had died in 1701 and his son, James Francis Edward, known as the Old Pretender, decided to re-establish the Stuart dynasty. By now William and Mary were dead and Britain was ruled by George, the first of the Hanoverian kings.

The Jacobites were a political movement dedicated to restoring the Stuarts to the throne. Their name came from "Jacobus", the Latin for James. They had formed a sizeable army to fight for the Old Pretender's cause.

In December 1715, James, who'd spent all but the first ten months of his life in France, finally set foot on Scottish soil. But by then his cause was all but lost. A month earlier a 12,000-

strong Jacobite army, led by the Earl of Mar, took on a government force half its size in the Battle of Sheriffmuir. The result was indecisive, with similar amounts of casualties on both sides. But it was a moral victory for the government and a major turning point in the rebellion. The leader of the smaller army was John Campbell, second Duke of Argyll, ably supported by his kinsmen, the MacCallums. Soon after his arrival James, disappointed by the strength of support he found, returned to the Continent and the rebellion ended. A second rebellion followed 30 years later and the consequences of this had long-lasting effects on the MacCallums.

James's first-born son, Charles Edward Stuart, became known as The Young Pretender, although he is romantically remembered as Bonnie Prince Charlie. He, too, attempted to regain the crown for his family. In July 1745 he landed with seven companions at Eriskay. He'd arrived in Scotland for the first time from Italy, where he'd spent almost all of his life. Charles had expected the support of the French fleet but it had been battered by storms and so he was left to raise an army on his own. The Jacobite cause was still supported by many Highland clans, both Catholic and Protestant, and the Catholic Charles was able to pull them together and raise an army. After initial successes, which took him all the way to Derby, The Jacobites found themselves facing King George II's son, the Duke of Cumberland, at the Battle of Culloden on April 16, 1746. His disastrous tactics led to a terrible defeat and the end of the Jacobite cause.

Charles escaped and made his way back to Italy where he saw out the remainder of his life. Highlanders had fought on both sides. In many cases relatives from the same family or clan opposed each other. Despite that, the government clamped down on the clan system with new laws. Severe civil penalties were introduced and Highland dress was outlawed.

It's unclear if the MacCallums were involved at Culloden as a clan. It's likely clan members may have fought on either side as individuals, but as Highlanders they were treated as roughly as those clans who did fight for the Jacobites. In order to avoid the worst of the repression the MacCallums decided to change their name yet again. The chief chose "Malcolm" and to this day the chief of the MacCallum clan is a Malcolm.

Chapter five:

Famous Davids

David McCallum was born in Glasgow, in 1933 but was educated in London, where his parents, both musicians, were based.

By the age of ten he was a radio regular with a talent for character voices. His parents wanted him to follow their career and initially he studied the oboe and French horn. But young David was more interested in acting and reluctantly it was agreed he could go to the Royal Academy of Dramatic Art. His acting career began with bit parts in British films in the 1950s. But in 1961 he headed to the US in the hope of breaking into the big time. His chance came when he was cast as Ilya Kuryakin in the hit TV show *The Man From UNCLE* alongside the more flamboyant Robert Vaughan who played Napoleon Solo. The pair "worked" for *United Network Command for Law Enforcement* and were involved in a constant battle against the

Technological Hierarchy for the Removal of Undesirables and Subjugation of Humanity, who were better known as the evil *THRUSH*. It ran from 1964 to 1968 and by its end David McCallum was an established star. He was also married to succeesful actress Jill Ireland. They had three sons, one of whom, Jason, was adopted. While filming *The Great Escape*, David introduced his wife to Charles Bronson, who was one of the stars in the movie. The film was released in 1963 and not long after Jill Ireland left him for Charles Bronson. The McCallums divorced in 1967 and David married Katherine Carpenter. They have two children and live in New York. Jill Ireland went on to marry Bronson the following year. Jason McCallum was then re-adopted by Ireland and Bronson but in 1989 tragically died of an overdose. Jill Ireland died of breast cancer in 1990. Thanks to the success of *The Man from UNCLE* McCallum starred in *The Big TNT Show*, introducing major acts like Ike and Tina Turner, Joan Baez and Ray Charles. He later enjoyed critical and commercial success back in Britain as part of the cast of *Colditz*, a Second World War POW series based on a true story.

David McCallum senior, was born in 1897 in Kilsyth, near Glasgow into a musical family. His mother, who played the organ, encouraged David to embrace a musical career and at the age of seven he took his first violin lesson. He then progressed to the Glasgow Academy of Music followed by a scholarship to the Royal College, London. By 1932 he was the leader of the Scottish Orchestra in Glasgow. This role is sometimes referred to as "concertmaster" who is the leader of the first violin section of a symphony orchestra. The leader usually plays the violin solos and makes decisions regarding technical details for the violins, and sometimes all of the string players. He or she is also in charge of leading the orchestra in tuning before concerts and rehearsals and plays a major role in the overall management of an orchestra. In 1936 McCallum accepted an invitation to lead the London Philharmonic Orchestra. During the Second World War he led the National Symphony

Orchestra and played with the London Studio Players and the BBC's Overseas Music Unit. After the war McCallum joined the Royal Philharmonic Orchestra as its leader and in 1950 toured America. By 1952 he led the London Symphony Orchestra. His career really took off when, in 1961, McCallum joined Mantovani's orchestra. Annunzio Paolo Mantovani was a popular conductor and entertainer in the "light orchestra" style. He is probably more associated with the light orchestra genre than any other person. For the next ten years McCallum led Mantovani's orchestra around the world as they toured America, Japan and Canada, as well as playing extensively in Britain and throughout Europe. David McCallum died in Sussex in March 1971. Throughout his career he never lost his Scottish accent and was rarely seen without a violin in his hand.

GATHERING OF THE CLANS

CLAN MEMORABILIA FROM LANG SYNE

Books, postcards, Teddy bears, keyrings, mugs and much more...

Visit our website:
www.langsyneshop.co.uk

or phone/write to us for a catalogue:
Lang Syne Publishing
Strathclyde Business Centre
120 Carstairs Street, Glasgow G40 4JD
Tel: 0141 554 9944 Fax: 0141 554 9955
E-mail: info@scottish-memories.co.uk